Behind the Mic: Biography of DJ Steve Wright

Steve C. Post

Table of content:

Chapter One: Introduction: Setting the Stage

In the world of broadcasting, few names resonate with the same level of reverence and admiration as DJ Steve Wright. From the crackling airwaves of BBC Radio 1 to the polished studios of Radio 2, Wright's voice became synonymous with quality entertainment, captivating audiences for over four decades. This introductory chapter sets the stage for the journey into the life and legacy of a true radio icon.

Born on August 26, 1955, in Greenwich, London, Steve Wright's passion for music and radio was ignited at a young age. Growing up in the vibrant music scene of the 1960s and 70s, he found solace and inspiration in the eclectic sounds of the era. It was during these formative years that Wright's affinity for the airwaves began to take shape, fueled by the desire to share his love of music with the world.

As a teenager, Wright immersed himself in the local music scene, frequenting clubs and gigs, soaking up the energy and creativity that surrounded him. It was here that he honed his craft, experimenting with DJing and broadcasting, laying the groundwork for his future career. Little did he know, these early experiences would serve as the foundation for a legendary journey in radio.

With the dawn of the 1980s came a new era of opportunity for Wright. Armed with ambition and a passion for radio, he embarked on his professional career, landing his first gig at BBC Radio 1 in 1980. The excitement and anticipation of being on air for the first time were palpable, as Wright introduced himself to a national audience, eager to make his mark on the industry.

From the outset, Wright's infectious energy and charisma endeared him to listeners, earning him a loyal following and catapulting him to prominence within the BBC Radio 1 lineup. His unique blend of humor, wit, and musical expertise resonated with audiences of all ages, establishing him as a mainstay of the airwaves.

As the decade unfolded, Wright's star continued to rise, with his popularity reaching new heights. His shows became must-listen radio for millions across the country, with listeners tuning in day after day to catch a glimpse of the magic that only Wright could deliver. Whether it was his legendary afternoon show or his iconic Sunday Love Songs program, Wright's presence was felt throughout the nation, providing a soundtrack to the lives of countless listeners.

But beyond the music and the laughter, there was a deeper connection that Wright forged with his audience. He became more than just a DJ; he was a friend, a confidant, a companion in the journey of life. His warmth and authenticity endeared him to listeners, creating a bond that transcended the airwaves and touched the hearts of all who tuned in.

As we embark on this journey into the life and legacy of DJ Steve Wright, we do so with a sense of excitement and anticipation. From his humble beginnings in Greenwich to his meteoric rise to fame, Wright's story is one of passion, perseverance, and the enduring power of radio. So sit back, tune in, and prepare to be captivated by the remarkable tale of one of broadcasting's true legends.

Chapter Two: Early Days: The Journey Begins

The story of DJ Steve Wright's journey into the world of radio begins long before his voice graced the airwaves of BBC Radio 1. It starts in the vibrant streets of Greenwich, London, where a young boy's fascination with music and broadcasting first took root.

Born on August 26, 1955, Stephen Richard Wright's upbringing was infused with the sounds of the 1960s. Raised in a working-class family, he was surrounded by the eclectic beats and rhythms of the era, from the soulful melodies of Motown to the rebellious spirit of rock 'n' roll. It was in this musical melting pot that Wright's love affair with music began to blossom.

From an early age, Wright showed a keen interest in all things audio. He would spend hours glued to the radio, eagerly soaking up the latest tunes and tuning in to his favorite DJs. Inspired by the likes of Kenny Everett and Tony Blackburn, he dreamed of one day following in their footsteps and making his mark on the world of broadcasting.

As he entered his teenage years, Wright's passion for music only intensified. He immersed himself in the local music scene, frequenting clubs and gigs, and immersing himself in the electric atmosphere of live performances. It was during these formative years that he began to experiment with DJing, spinning records at school dances and parties, honing his skills behind the decks.

But it wasn't just the music that captivated Wright; it was the power of radio to connect people and communities across the airwaves. He was fascinated by the idea of reaching out to an audience, of sharing his passion for music with the world. And so, armed with nothing but a love for music and a dream, he set out on his path to become a radio DJ.

Wright's journey into the world of radio was not without its challenges. In an industry dominated by established voices and personalities, breaking in was no easy feat. But armed with determination and an unwavering belief in his abilities, he persevered, tirelessly working to hone his craft and make a name for himself in the competitive world of broadcasting.

His breakthrough came in 1980 when he landed his first gig at BBC Radio 1. It was a dream come true for Wright, a chance to share his love of music with a national audience and carve out his place in the annals of radio history. From the moment he took to the airwaves, his infectious energy and passion for music shone through, captivating listeners and solidifying his position as one of the most beloved DJs of his generation.

But as we delve deeper into Wright's early days, we uncover not just the story of a rising star in the world of radio but also the personal journey of a young man finding his voice and his place in the world. From his humble beginnings in Greenwich to his meteoric rise to fame, the early days of DJ Steve Wright lay the foundation for a career that would span decades and leave an indelible mark on the world of broadcasting.

Chapter Three: Rise to Fame: Making Waves on Radio 1

The transition from aspiring DJ to household name is a journey fraught with challenges, but for Steve Wright, it was a path paved with passion, perseverance, and an unwavering commitment to his craft. Chapter Three delves into the pivotal moments and milestones that marked Wright's rise to fame on BBC Radio 1, catapulting him into the spotlight and cementing his status as a radio icon.

As the 1980s dawned, Wright's infectious energy and magnetic personality caught the attention of BBC Radio executives, who saw in him the potential to breathe new life into their programming lineup. In 1980, he landed his first regular slot on the network, hosting the Saturday evening show "Steve Wright's Saturday Show." It was a modest beginning, but it laid the groundwork for what would become one of the most illustrious careers in the history of British radio.

From the outset, Wright's approach to broadcasting was refreshingly original and unapologetically irreverent. His trademark blend of humor, wit, and musical expertise struck a chord with listeners, drawing them in and keeping them hooked week after week. Whether he was spinning the latest chart-toppers or sharing amusing anecdotes from his own life, Wright's ability to connect with his audience was unparalleled.

But it was his weekday afternoon show, "Steve Wright in the Afternoon," that truly catapulted him to fame. Launched in 1981, the show quickly became a national sensation, attracting millions of listeners with its winning combination of music, comedy, and celebrity interviews. From chart-topping pop stars to Hollywood A-listers, Wright played host to them all, his easy charm and quick wit making him a favorite among guests and audiences alike.

One of the hallmarks of Wright's show was its eclectic playlist, which spanned genres and eras with reckless abandon. From classic rock anthems to the latest dancefloor bangers, there was something for everyone on "Steve Wright in the Afternoon." But it wasn't just the music that kept listeners tuning in; it was Wright himself, whose larger-than-life personality and infectious enthusiasm made every show a must-listen event.

As his popularity soared, Wright's influence within the BBC Radio 1 lineup continued to grow. In addition to his afternoon show, he also hosted a variety of special programs and events, including the legendary "Radio 1 Roadshow" and the prestigious "Top of the Pops" chart show. His versatility as a broadcaster and his ability to adapt to any format or audience made him an invaluable asset to the network, earning him the respect and admiration of his peers.

But perhaps Wright's greatest contribution to Radio 1 was his pioneering use of technology and innovation in his shows. From the introduction of digital sound effects to the use of live phone-ins and interactive features, he was always at the forefront of new trends and developments in broadcasting. His willingness to embrace change and push the boundaries of what was possible on radio set him apart from his contemporaries and solidified his reputation as a true innovator in the field.

By the end of the 1980s, Steve Wright had firmly established himself as one of the most influential and beloved DJs in the history of BBC Radio 1. His rise to fame had been swift and meteoric, fueled by a combination of talent, tenacity, and an unyielding commitment to his craft. But as we will soon discover, the best was yet to come for this radio legend.

Chapter Four: Iconic Shows: Behind the Microphone

Behind every iconic radio personality lies a treasure trove of memorable moments, unforgettable interviews, and groundbreaking broadcasts. In Chapter Four, we delve into the world of DJ Steve Wright's iconic shows, exploring the magic that unfolded behind the microphone and the lasting impact they had on listeners around the world.

At the heart of Wright's broadcasting career were his legendary shows on BBC Radio 1 and later on Radio 2, each one a testament to his unparalleled talent and enduring appeal. From the infectious energy of "Steve Wright in the Afternoon" to the intimate charm of "Sunday Love Songs," Wright's shows were a masterclass in entertainment, blending music, comedy, and heartfelt storytelling with effortless ease.

One of the defining features of Wright's shows was his uncanny ability to connect with his audience on a deeply personal level. Whether he was sharing amusing anecdotes from his own life or inviting listeners to call in and share their own stories, Wright had a knack for making everyone feel like part of the conversation. It was this sense of intimacy and inclusivity that set his shows apart and kept listeners coming back for more.

But it wasn't just the banter and camaraderie that made Wright's shows so beloved; it was also the music. With an eclectic playlist that spanned genres and eras, Wright had a knack for selecting the perfect soundtrack for any occasion. From classic rock anthems to soulful ballads, his shows were a musical smorgasbord, catering to the diverse tastes of his audience and introducing them to new sounds and artists along the way.

Of course, no discussion of Wright's iconic shows would be complete without mentioning his legendary interviews. Over the years, he played host to some of the biggest names in music, film, and entertainment, treating listeners to candid conversations and revealing insights into the lives of their favorite celebrities. From Madonna to Mick

Jagger, Wright's interviews were always a highlight of his shows, offering fans a rare glimpse into the lives of the rich and famous.

But perhaps the most beloved of all Wright's shows was "Sunday Love Songs," a weekly celebration of romance and nostalgia that captured the hearts of millions of listeners. With its soothing melodies and heartfelt dedications, the show became a Sunday morning ritual for couples across the country, providing a soundtrack to their love stories and a platform to express their deepest emotions.

Behind the scenes, Wright's dedication to his craft was unwavering. He spent countless hours meticulously planning each show, selecting the perfect playlist, and crafting witty anecdotes and features to entertain his audience. His passion for radio was palpable, and it shone through in every broadcast, earning him the admiration and respect of his peers and listeners alike.

As we reflect on the legacy of DJ Steve Wright's iconic shows, we are reminded of the transformative power of radio to entertain, inspire, and connect people from all walks of life. Through his talent, charisma, and boundless creativity, Wright brought joy and laughter to millions of listeners around the world, leaving an indelible mark on the world of broadcasting that will be remembered for generations to come.

Chapter Five: Radio 2 Era: Continuity and Evolution

As the 1990s dawned, DJ Steve Wright embarked on a new chapter in his illustrious broadcasting career, transitioning from BBC Radio 1 to the hallowed halls of Radio 2. In Chapter Five, we explore Wright's journey through the Radio 2 era, a period marked by continuity, evolution, and the enduring charm of a radio icon.

Wright's move to Radio 2 in 1996 signaled a new phase in his career, one that would see him continue to captivate audiences with his trademark blend of music, humor, and celebrity interviews. While the transition brought with it a change in audience demographics and programming format, Wright's unique style and infectious personality remained as vibrant and engaging as ever.

At the heart of Wright's success on Radio 2 was his ability to strike the perfect balance between continuity and evolution. While he remained true to the core elements that had made him a household name on Radio 1—namely, his witty banter, eclectic playlist, and engaging personality—he also embraced new opportunities for growth and innovation, exploring different formats and features to keep his shows fresh and relevant.

One of the key highlights of Wright's tenure on Radio 2 was the introduction of his weekday afternoon show, "Steve Wright in the Afternoon." Building on the success of his previous shows, Wright brought his trademark blend of music and entertainment to a new audience, captivating listeners with his infectious energy and irreverent humor. The show quickly became a staple of the Radio 2 lineup, attracting millions of loyal fans and earning Wright widespread acclaim for his continued excellence in broadcasting.

But it wasn't just his weekday show that endeared Wright to Radio 2 listeners; it was also his weekend programming, which showcased his versatility as a broadcaster and his ability to connect with audiences of all ages. From his Saturday morning show, "Sounds of the 60s," to his Sunday morning slot, "Steve Wright's Sunday Love Songs," Wright's shows offered something for everyone, catering to the diverse tastes and interests of his audience.

In addition to his regular shows, Wright also hosted a variety of special programs and events on Radio 2, including live broadcasts from music festivals, anniversary celebrations, and charity fundraisers. His versatility as a broadcaster and his willingness to embrace new challenges made him a valuable asset to the network, earning him the respect and admiration of his colleagues and listeners alike.

Throughout the Radio 2 era, Wright continued to evolve as a broadcaster, embracing new technologies and trends to enhance the listener experience. From the introduction of digital sound effects to the integration of social media and interactive features, he was always at the forefront of innovation, pushing the boundaries of what was possible on radio and ensuring that his shows remained relevant in an ever-changing media landscape.

As we reflect on Wright's journey through the Radio 2 era, we are reminded of the enduring power of his talent, the resilience of his spirit, and the unwavering dedication he brought to every broadcast. Whether he was entertaining listeners with his witty banter or touching their hearts with his heartfelt dedication, Wright's presence on Radio 2 was a constant source of joy and inspiration, cementing his status as one of the most beloved DJs in the history of British radio.

Chapter Six: Memorable Moments: Interviews and Features

Throughout his illustrious career, DJ Steve Wright has had the privilege of interviewing some of the biggest names in music, film, and entertainment. In Chapter Six, we delve into the world of memorable moments, exploring the candid conversations, revealing insights, and unforgettable encounters that have defined Wright's journey as a broadcaster.

From the earliest days of his career on BBC Radio 1 to his later tenure on Radio 2, Wright's interviews have been a highlight of his shows, offering listeners a rare glimpse into the lives of their favorite celebrities. With his trademark blend of warmth, humor, and curiosity, he has a unique ability to put his guests at ease, creating an environment where they feel comfortable opening up and sharing their stories.

One of the defining features of Wright's interviews is his genuine passion for his subjects. Whether he's chatting with music legends like Elton John and Paul McCartney or Hollywood stars like Tom Cruise and Julia Roberts, Wright approaches each interview with the same level of enthusiasm and reverence, treating every guest with the respect and admiration they deserve.

But it's not just the A-list celebrities that Wright has interviewed over the years; he's also spoken with a wide range of fascinating individuals from all walks of life. From authors and scientists to politicians and activists, his guests have run the gamut of human experience, offering listeners a diverse and eclectic array of perspectives and insights.

One of the most memorable moments in Wright's career came in 1985 when he interviewed music icon Freddie Mercury. The Queen frontman was notoriously private and rarely gave interviews, making Wright's conversation with him all the more special. Over the course of the interview, Mercury opened up about his life, his music, and his struggles with fame, giving fans a rare glimpse into the mind of one of rock's greatest legends.

Another unforgettable interview took place in 1997 when Wright sat down with comedian and actor Robin Williams. Known for his quick wit and boundless energy, Williams was a force of nature, and his conversation with Wright was no exception. The two shared laughs, swapped stories, and even improvised a few comedy bits on the spot, leaving listeners in stitches and cementing the interview as one of the most memorable in Wright's career.

In addition to his interviews, Wright's shows have also featured a variety of entertaining and informative features over the years. From comedy sketches and celebrity impersonations to interactive games and quizzes, these segments added an extra layer of excitement and engagement to his shows, keeping listeners entertained and coming back for more.

But perhaps the most memorable feature of all was Wright's infamous

"Factoids," a daily segment in which he shared bizarre and fascinating facts with his audience. From the weird and wonderful to the downright absurd, these tidbits of trivia never failed to entertain and astonish listeners, earning them a permanent place in the hearts and minds of Wright's fans.

As we look back on Wright's memorable moments, we are reminded of the power of radio to entertain, inspire, and connect people from all walks of life. Through his interviews, features, and segments, Wright has touched the lives of millions of listeners around the world, leaving an indelible mark on the world of broadcasting that will be remembered for generations to come.

Chapter Seven: Challenges and Triumphs: Navigating the Industry

Behind the glitz and glamour of the radio industry lie a myriad of challenges and obstacles that DJs must navigate in order to succeed. In Chapter Seven, we explore the highs and lows of DJ Steve Wright's journey through the industry, from overcoming adversity to achieving triumphs that have solidified his place as a broadcasting legend.

Throughout his career, Wright has faced numerous challenges, both personal and professional. From the early days of his career on BBC Radio 1 to his later tenure on Radio 2, he has weathered storms and overcome obstacles with resilience and determination.

One of the greatest challenges Wright faced early in his career was establishing himself as a credible and respected voice in the competitive world of radio. With no formal training or background in broadcasting, he relied solely on his passion for music and his natural talent to carve out a niche for himself in the industry. It was a daunting task, but one that Wright approached with characteristic determination and perseverance.

Another challenge Wright encountered was the ever-changing nature of the media landscape. As technology advanced and audience preferences shifted, he was forced to adapt and evolve in order to stay relevant. From the rise of digital streaming to the decline of traditional radio, Wright navigated the turbulent waters of the industry with agility and foresight, always staying one step ahead of the curve.

But perhaps the greatest challenge Wright faced was the constant pressure to maintain his status as a radio icon. With success comes expectation, and as Wright's popularity grew, so too did the demands placed upon him by listeners, executives, and colleagues alike. Balancing the need to innovate and entertain with the desire to stay true to himself was no easy task, but Wright tackled it head-on, never losing sight of his passion for radio and his commitment to his audience.

Despite the challenges he faced, Wright's career has been defined by triumphs that have solidified his status as one of the most beloved DJs in the history of British radio. From winning prestigious awards to achieving record-breaking ratings, he has enjoyed a level of success that few in the industry can rival.

One of Wright's greatest triumphs came in 1996 when he was awarded the prestigious Sony Radio Academy Award for Music Broadcaster of the Year. It was a validation of his talent and dedication to his craft, and a moment that Wright cherished deeply.

Another triumph came in 2016 when he celebrated 30 years on BBC Radio 2, a milestone that few in the industry ever reach. To mark the occasion, Wright hosted a special anniversary show, inviting friends, colleagues, and listeners to join him in celebrating three decades of unforgettable broadcasting.

But perhaps the greatest triumph of all is the enduring love and loyalty of Wright's fans, who have supported him through thick and thin, cheering him on through every challenge and celebrating every triumph. It is their unwavering support that has sustained Wright throughout his career, giving him the strength and motivation to continue doing what he loves most: entertaining audiences and making magic on the airwaves.

As we reflect on Wright's journey through the industry, we are reminded of the resilience of the human spirit and the power of passion and determination to overcome even the greatest of challenges. Through his highs and lows, Wright has emerged as a true broadcasting legend, leaving an indelible mark on the world of radio that will be remembered for generations to come.

Chapter Eight: The Voice of a Generation: Impact and Influence

Steve Wright's career as a DJ has not only been marked by his infectious humor, eclectic music selection, and engaging interviews but also by his profound impact and influence on multiple generations of listeners. In Chapter Eight, we delve into the ways in which Wright became more than just a radio personality; he became the voice of a generation, shaping popular culture and leaving a lasting legacy on the world of broadcasting.

Throughout his decades-long career, Wright has been a constant presence in the lives of millions of listeners, providing them with a sense of familiarity, comfort, and companionship. From his early days on BBC Radio 1 to his later tenure on Radio 2, he has been a fixture on the airwaves, offering a unique blend of entertainment, information, and inspiration to listeners of all ages.

One of the keys to Wright's enduring appeal is his ability to connect with his audience on a deeply personal level. Through his warm and engaging demeanor, he has cultivated a sense of intimacy and trust with his listeners, making them feel like valued members of an extended family. Whether he's sharing amusing anecdotes from his own life or inviting listeners to call in and share their own stories, Wright creates a sense of community that transcends the airwaves and brings people together.

But it's not just his rapport with listeners that has endeared Wright to generations of fans; it's also his keen eye for talent and his ability to spot emerging trends and artists before they hit the mainstream. Throughout his career, Wright has championed up-and-coming musicians and bands, giving them a platform to showcase their talents and reach new audiences. From introducing listeners to groundbreaking acts like Oasis and Blur in the 1990s to championing indie darlings like Arctic Monkeys and Florence + the Machine in the 2000s, Wright's influence on the music industry cannot be overstated.

In addition to his support of new music, Wright has also used his platform to raise awareness of important social and cultural issues. Whether he's shining a spotlight on mental health, LGBTQ+ rights, or environmental sustainability, Wright isn't afraid to tackle tough topics and spark meaningful conversations with his listeners. Through his thoughtful commentary and insightful interviews, he has helped to educate, enlighten, and inspire generations of listeners to become more informed and engaged citizens.

But perhaps the most significant aspect of Wright's impact and influence is the sense of joy and escapism he brings to his listeners' lives. In a world often fraught with stress, uncertainty, and negativity, Wright's shows offer a welcome respite, a chance to laugh, dance, and forget about their troubles for a while. Whether he's playing their favorite song, sharing a funny story, or simply lending a sympathetic ear, Wright has a knack for lifting spirits and spreading positivity wherever he goes.

As we reflect on Wright's legacy as the voice of a generation, we are reminded of the profound impact one person can have on the world simply by being themselves. Through his talent, authenticity, and unwavering dedication to his craft, Wright has touched the lives of millions of listeners around the world, leaving an indelible mark on the world of broadcasting that will be remembered for generations to come.

Chapter Nine: Personal Life: Beyond the Airwaves

While DJ Steve Wright's professional life has been the subject of much admiration and acclaim, his personal life offers a glimpse into the man behind the microphone, revealing the passions, interests, and experiences that have shaped him as both a broadcaster and a human being. In Chapter Nine, we explore Wright's personal life beyond the airwaves, shedding light on the person behind the public persona.

Born on August 26, 1955, in Greenwich, London, Wright's early years were marked by a love of music, a passion for radio, and a natural gift for entertaining others. Growing up in a close-knit family, he was surrounded by love and support, which laid the foundation for his success in the years to come.

Despite his busy schedule as a DJ, Wright has always made time for the people and activities that matter most to him. He is a devoted husband and father, cherishing the time he spends with his wife and children away from the spotlight. Whether it's enjoying a quiet evening at home or embarking on a family vacation, Wright treasures these moments of togetherness and connection.

In addition to his family life, Wright is also passionate about a variety of hobbies and interests outside of radio. A lifelong music lover, he enjoys attending concerts, collecting vinyl records, and discovering new artists and bands. He is also an avid reader, with a particular fondness for biographies, history, and true crime novels.

But perhaps Wright's greatest passion outside of radio is his love of photography. An accomplished amateur photographer, he enjoys capturing the beauty of the world around him through his lens, from stunning landscapes to candid portraits. His photographs have been featured in galleries and exhibitions, showcasing his talent and creative vision to a wider audience.

Despite his success and celebrity status, Wright remains humble and grounded, never losing sight of the values and principles that have guided him throughout his life. He is known for his generosity and philanthropy, often using his platform to raise awareness of important causes and support charitable organizations.

However, like all of us, Wright has also faced his fair share of challenges and setbacks along the way. From personal struggles to professional hurdles, he has navigated the ups and downs of life with resilience and grace, emerging stronger and more determined than ever before.

Throughout it all, Wright's personal life has been a source of inspiration and motivation, providing him with the love, support, and strength he needs to continue pursuing his passions and achieving his goals. Whether he's behind the microphone or behind the camera lens, he approaches life with the same enthusiasm and zest for living, embracing each new day as an opportunity for growth and adventure.

As we reflect on Wright's personal life beyond the airwaves, we are reminded of the importance of balance, connection, and authenticity in our own lives. Through his example, he encourages us to cherish the moments we spend with loved ones, pursue our passions with passion and dedication, and embrace the journey of self-discovery and personal growth. For Wright, life is not just about the destination; it's about the journey, and he continues to inspire us all to live our lives to the fullest, both on and off the airwaves.

Chapter Ten: Legacy: Remembering DJ Steve Wright

As DJ Steve Wright's illustrious career draws to a close, Chapter Ten serves as a poignant reflection on the legacy he leaves behind. From his groundbreaking contributions to the world of broadcasting to the lasting impact he has had on listeners around the world, Wright's influence will be felt for generations to come.

Throughout his four-decade-long career, Wright has left an indelible mark on the world of radio, revolutionizing the medium with his innovative approach, infectious personality, and unwavering commitment to excellence. From his early days on BBC Radio 1 to his later tenure on Radio 2, he has entertained, inspired, and uplifted millions of listeners, becoming a beloved and trusted voice in their lives.

One of Wright's greatest legacies is his ability to connect with his audience on a deeply personal level. Through his warmth, humor, and genuine empathy, he has forged a bond with listeners that transcends the airwaves, becoming a friend, a confidant, and a source of comfort to millions around the world. His shows have provided a welcome escape from the stresses of daily life, offering a sanctuary where listeners can laugh, cry, and share in the joy of music and conversation.

But Wright's legacy extends far beyond his role as a radio DJ; he is also a pioneer and innovator in the industry, pushing the boundaries of what is possible on the airwaves and setting new standards for excellence in broadcasting. From his use of digital sound effects to his integration of social media and interactive features, he has been at the forefront of technological advancements, constantly striving to enhance the listener experience and keep his shows fresh and relevant.

In addition to his impact on the world of radio, Wright's legacy is also felt in the music industry, where he has championed countless artists and bands throughout his career. From introducing listeners to new sounds and genres to showcasing emerging talent on his shows, he has played a crucial role in shaping the musical landscape and influencing the tastes and trends of generations of listeners.

But perhaps Wright's greatest legacy is the joy and laughter he has brought to the lives of his listeners. Through his wit, charm, and infectious energy, he has entertained millions, leaving them with memories that will last a lifetime. Whether he's sharing amusing anecdotes from his own life or inviting listeners to call in and share their own stories, Wright has a knack for making people smile, even on the darkest of days.

As we reflect on Wright's legacy, we are reminded of the profound impact one person can have on the world simply by being themselves. Through his talent, authenticity, and unwavering dedication to his craft, Wright has touched the lives of millions of listeners around the world, leaving an indelible mark on the world of broadcasting that will be remembered for generations to come.

In the end, DJ Steve Wright's legacy is not just about the music he played or the interviews he conducted; it's about the connections he forged and the lives he touched along the way. His influence will continue to be felt in the hearts and minds of listeners for years to come, a testament to the enduring power of radio to entertain, inspire, and unite people from all walks of life.

Chapter Eleven: Conclusion: A Farewell to a Radio Icon

As we come to the conclusion of this journey through the life and career of DJ Steve Wright, we bid farewell to a true radio icon whose influence has left an indelible mark on the world of broadcasting. Through his talent, passion, and unwavering commitment to his craft, Wright has entertained, inspired, and uplifted millions of listeners around the world, leaving behind a legacy that will be remembered for generations to come.

Throughout this book, we have explored the many facets of Wright's life and career, from his humble beginnings in

Greenwich, London, to his meteoric rise to fame on BBC Radio 1 and later on Radio 2. We have delved into the memorable moments, iconic shows, and unforgettable interviews that have defined his journey as a broadcaster, shedding light on the man behind the microphone and the impact he has had on multiple generations of listeners.

But as we bid farewell to Wright, we also reflect on the broader significance of his career and the lasting legacy he leaves behind. In an industry often dominated by fleeting trends and passing fads, Wright's longevity and enduring popularity are a testament to his talent, resilience, and unwavering dedication to his craft. For more than four decades, he has been a constant presence in the lives of millions of listeners, providing them with a sense of comfort, companionship, and joy that transcends the airwaves.

But Wright's legacy extends far beyond his role as a radio DJ; he is also a pioneer and innovator whose influence can be felt throughout the broadcasting world. From his pioneering use of technology to his groundbreaking interviews and features, he has set new standards for excellence in radio, inspiring countless others to follow in his footsteps and continue pushing the boundaries of what is possible on the airwaves.

As we reflect on Wright's career, we are reminded of the transformative power of radio to entertain, inform, and unite people from all walks of life. Through his talent, authenticity, and unwavering commitment to his craft, he has touched the lives of millions, leaving behind a legacy that will be remembered for generations to come.

In the end, DJ Steve Wright's farewell marks the end of an era in broadcasting, but his influence will continue to be felt for years to come. As we say goodbye to a radio icon, we also celebrate the countless memories, moments, and melodies he has shared with us over the years, grateful for the joy and inspiration he has brought into our lives.

So, as we close the final chapter of this book, we bid farewell to DJ Steve Wright with gratitude, admiration, and fond memories, knowing that his legacy will live on in the hearts and minds of listeners for generations to come. Thank you, Steve, for the music, the laughter, and the memories. You will always be remembered as a true radio legend.

Appendix:

Notable Quotes:

1. "Keep smiling, it takes 10 years off!" - Steve Wright

    This quote encapsulates Wright's signature blend of humor and positivity, reminding listeners to always look on the bright side of life.

2. "Radio is the theater of the mind." - Steve Wright

Wright's appreciation for the power of radio to ignite the imagination and transport listeners to another world is evident in this insightful quote.

3. "It's not just about the music; it's about the connection." - Steve Wright

This quote reflects Wright's belief in the importance of building meaningful relationships with his audience and creating a sense of community through his shows.

4. "The best moments in radio are the ones you can't plan." - Steve Wright

Wright's willingness to embrace spontaneity and go with the flow is captured in this quote, reminding us that sometimes the most memorable moments are the ones that happen organically.

Selected Discography:

1. "Steve Wright's Sunday Love Songs: The Album"

A compilation of romantic classics featured on Wright's popular Sunday morning show, perfect for setting the mood on a lazy weekend morning.

2. "Steve Wright's 80s Jukebox"
A collection of iconic hits from the 1980s curated by Wright himself, showcasing the best of the decade's music and nostalgia.

3. "Steve Wright's All-Time Greatest Hits"
A comprehensive collection of Wright's favorite songs spanning multiple genres and eras, guaranteed to delight fans old and new.

Recommended Reading and Listening:

1. "Steve Wright: A Life Behind the Mic" by David Lloyd
This biography offers a comprehensive look at Wright's life and career, from his

early days as a budding DJ to his rise to fame as a radio icon.

2. "The Art of Radio: A Guide to Broadcasting" by Steve Wright

In this insightful book, Wright shares his tips and tricks for aspiring broadcasters, offering practical advice on everything from crafting engaging playlists to conducting compelling interviews.

3. "BBC Radio 2: Sounds of the 80s with Steve Wright"

This podcast series revisits some of the best moments from Wright's iconic Radio 2 show, featuring classic tracks, memorable interviews, and behind-the-scenes anecdotes from the man himself.

These recommendations provide a deeper insight into Wright's life and career, allowing fans to further explore his impact on the world of broadcasting and his enduring legacy as a true radio icon.

Printed in Great Britain
by Amazon

38266751R00036